Classifying Fish

RICHARD AND LOUISE SPILSBURY

Heinemann
LIBRARY

www.heinemann.co.uk/library
Visit our website to find out more information about **Heinemann Library** books.

To order:
☎ Phone 44 (0) 1865 888066
🖹 Send a fax to 44 (0) 1865 314091
🖥 Visit the Heinemann Bookshop at www.heinemann.co.uk/library to browse our catalogue and order online.

First published in Great Britain by Heinemann Library, Halley Court, Jordan Hill, Oxford OX2 8EJ, part of Harcourt Education. Heinemann is a registered trademark of Harcourt Education Ltd.

Editorial: Jilly Attwood and Jennifer Tubbs
Design: Jo Hinton-Malivoire and AMR
Illustrations: David Woodroffe
Picture Research: Catherine Bevan, Hannah Taylor and Su Alexander
Production: Séverine Ribierre

Originated by Dot Gradations Ltd
Printed in China

ISBN 0 431 16784 2 (hardback)
07 06 05 04 03
10 9 8 7 6 5 4 3 2 1

ISBN 0 431 16791 5 (paperback)
08 07 06 05 04
10 9 8 7 6 5 4 3 2 1

British Library Cataloguing in Publication Data
Spilsbury, Richard and Louise
Classifying Living Things – Fish
597'.012
A full catalogue record for this book is available from the British Library.

Acknowledgements
For Harriet and Miles, rock pool enthusiasts.

The publishers would like to thank the following for permission to reproduce photographs: Bruce Coleman: **4** (Franco Banfi), **28** (Pacific Stock); Corbis: **27** (Brandon D. Cole); Harcourt Index: **17**; Nature Picture Library: **8** (top) (Jeff Rotman), **8** (bottom) (Steve Packham), **9** (Avi Klapfer/Jeff Rotman), **10** (Jurgen Freund), **14** (Juan Manuel Borrero), **18** (Doug Allan), **19** (Dan Burton), **22** (Doc White), **24** (Jeff Rotman), **25** (Avi Klapfer/Jeff Rotman); NHPA: **23** (Norbert Wu); Oxford Scientific Films: **6** (P. Kent), **11** (Paulo De Oliviera), **12** (Colin Milkins), **13** (Richard Herrmann), **15** (Paul Kay), **16** (Rodger Jackman), **20** (Paul Kay), **21** (Rudie Kuiter), **26** (Norbert Wu), **29** (Howard Hall).

Cover photograph of soldier fish and butterfly fish reproduced with permission of Oxford Scientific Films.

The publishers would like to thank Martin Lawrence, museum educator, for his assistance in the preparation of this book.

Every effort has been made to contact copyright holders of any material reproduced in this book. Any omissions will be rectified in subsequent printings if notice is given to the publishers.

Contents

Words in the text in bold, **like this**, are explained in the Glossary.

How classification works

The Earth is populated with an immense variety of living things, from the largest whale to the tiniest insect. Scientists believe that all these **organisms** (living things) are the **descendants** of one group of simple organisms that lived millions of years ago. Classification can help us to understand how different organisms might be related to each other. It also makes better sense of the great variety of organisms by sorting them into groups.

Sorting life

Different living things are grouped according to the characteristics (features) that they have in common. Some are obvious at first glance. For example, any animal you see with feathers is a bird.

There are many hidden characteristics used to classify organisms. Fish, mammals, reptiles, birds and amphibians are classified together as **vertebrates** because they all have an internal backbone. Other less obvious characteristics used to classify include ways of **reproducing** (having babies), ways of breathing and types of skin.

There are many different ways to classify. Although scientists often disagree about the best ways, over time, they have come up with an agreed system of sorting all organisms.

The whale shark looks like a whale but it is a fish – it has characteristics in common with all other sorts of fish.

From kingdoms to species

Living things are divided into huge groups called kingdoms. Plants, for example, are all grouped in one kingdom, and all animals in another. Each kingdom is divided into smaller groups called **phyla** (singular phylum). A phylum contains several **classes**: classes contain **orders**; orders contain **families**; families contain **genera** (singular genus) and genera contain **species**. A species is a single kind of organism such as a hammerhead shark.

Common and scientific names

Many living things have a common name. Common names such as mackerel are not always exact – for instance, an American mackerel is different from an Indian mackerel.

To sort out difficulties like these, scientists give every species a two-part name. The first part of the name tells you the genus the organism belongs to. The second part is the name of the species within that genus.

Using scientific names, it is easy to tell the two types of mackerel apart. The American mackerel has the name *Scomber japonicus* and the Indian mackerel is *Rastrelliger kanagurta*.

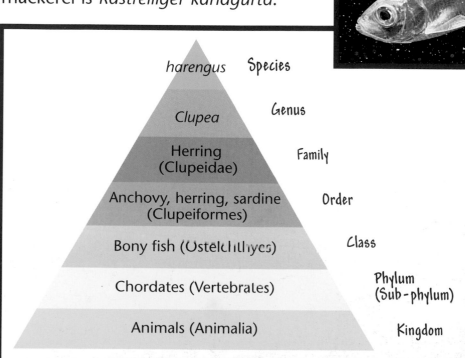

harengus	Species
Clupea	Genus
Herring (Clupeidae)	Family
Anchovy, herring, sardine (Clupeiformes)	Order
Bony fish (Osteichthyes)	Class
Chordates (Vertebrates)	Phylum (Sub-phylum)
Animals (Animalia)	Kingdom

This diagram shows the full classification for Clupea harengus – a herring.

What are fish?

Fish are **vertebrates** that live in water. Some live in seawater, others in freshwater, and some move from one to the other at different times in their lifecycle. Most use **fins** to swim.

Fish breathe using special parts of their body, called **gills**. They are generally cold-blooded, which means their bodies stay the same temperature as the water around them. Their skin is usually covered with protective **scales**. Finally, all fish **reproduce** using soft eggs that do not have shells.

All other animals that live in water differ from fish in some ways. For example, although dolphins live in water, are vertebrates and have fins just like fish, they are mammals because they are warm-blooded and **suckle** their young.

Classifying fish

The most important characteristics used in fish classification are the type of bone in their skeleton, type of gill structure, number and shape of fins and type of scales. Fish are usually sorted into three classes: jawless, **cartilaginous** and bony.

Jawless fish (class Agnatha) have no jaws and their skeletons are soft – made of cartilage not bone. Examples include lamprey and hagfish. Jawless fish are thought to be similar to some of the first types of fish that ever lived on Earth. The chart shows the two orders of jawless fish.

Lampreys are one of the two classes of jawless fish. Their circular sucking mouth is used to feed on the blood of other animals

Cartilaginous fish (class Chondrichthyes) have full cartilage skeletons (including jaws), pointed scales and gills that can be seen through gill slits on either side of their body. This class includes sharks, skates and rays. There are three orders of cartilaginous fish.

Bony fish (class Osteichthyes) have skeletons made of bone, flat scales and their gills are protected by gill covers. Over 90 per cent of all fish on Earth are bony fish. Examples include goldfish, cod and eels. Although there are 49 **orders** of bony fish, the chart gives the 15 best-known.

This table shows a selection of fish orders.

Fish class	Order	No. of species	Examples
Jawless fish	Lampreys (Petromyzoniformes)	25	Lamprey
	Hagfish (Myxiniformes)	20	Hagfish
Cartilaginous fish	Sharks (Selachii)	450	Great white shark
	Rays and skates (Rajiformes)	350	Manta ray
	Ratfish (Chimaeriformes)	25	Chimaera
Bony fish	Lungfish (Dipteriformes)	5	African lungfish
	Sturgeons (Acipenseriformes)	25	Sturgeon
	Eels (Anguilliformes)	300	Freshwater eel
	Herrings (Clupeiformes)	350	Anchovy, herring
	Carp (Cypriniformes)	350	Minnow, carp, piranha
	Salmon (Salmoniformes)	500	Trout, pike
	Catfish (Siluriformes)	2,210	Wels
	Anglers (Lophiiformes)	150	Batfish, goosefish
	Cod (Gadiformes)	450	Cod, hake, haddock
	Flying fish (Atheriniformes)	600	Flying fish, garfish, topminnow
	Seahorses (Gasterosteiformes)	150	Seahorse, sticklebacks, pipefish
	Scorpionfish (Scorpaeniformes)	700	Lionfish, sculpin
	Perch (Perciformes)	6,500	Perch, tuna, bass, blennies
	Flatfish (Pleuronectiformes)	500	Turbot, plaice, sole
	Boxfish (Tetraodontiformes)	250	Sunfish, pufferfish

Looking at fish

Some fish look like huge whales or spiky balloons, and others are as flat as frisbees. Many are silver but others are brightly coloured, spotted or striped. Regardless of how different they look on the outside, on the inside fish have a lot in common.

On the inside

On the inside, every fish has a skeleton including a backbone. Most fish have hard bones, but the bones of some fish are made of flexible **cartilage** – the same stuff that makes your ears and the tip of your nose hard but bendy.

Bones protect the fish's brain, its eyes and other important **organs** from damage. Some bones do not move, but others do, helped by muscles. For example, muscles open and close a fish's jaw bones.

Fish scales

Fish skin is usually covered by a protective layer of differently shaped transparent **scales**. Scales can be round and smooth on eels, but pointed and rough as sandpaper on sharks.

The trunk fish (above) has scales that fit together like a bony box to protect it. The carp (right) has overlapping smooth scales, a bit like roof tiles, that help it to swim fast.

Sailfish are the fastest swimmers of all fish, moving at up to 100 kilometres an hour.

Swimming

Fish have moveable **fins** (flaps of skin) that help them move through water. Bones in fins act like the struts in an umbrella to open and close the flap.

Most fins are used to steer, brake and balance in the water. Many fish have a pair of fins behind their eyes – the **pectoral** fins – and fins on their back – the **dorsal** fins. Fish such as sharks usually have a tall dorsal fin, but others such as eels have a long, narrow dorsal fin.

The tail fin is used to move through the water. Rows of muscles along the backbone twist the tail from side to side. The tail fin then moves the water behind the fish out of the way and it goes forward. Most fish have tail fins that are symmetrical (the same top and bottom). Ocean swimmers, such as sailfish or flying fish, have crescent-shaped tail fins that help them go faster.

Shaped for swimming

Most fish have a smooth streamlined shape – they are pointed at either end so that water can flow quickly over them. This is often helped by smooth scales and by slime on the skin. Many fish tuck their fins in when they want to go even faster.

Living underwater

All fish have **gills** to breathe with underwater. Amphibians (frogs, toads and newts) breathe using gills when they are young, but as they grow up they start to breathe with lungs or through their skin. Fish never have lungs – they have gills throughout their lives.

Catching a breath

Gills contain lots of thin blood vessels (tubes). As water moves over the gills, oxygen (a gas dissolved in the water) moves from the water to blood in these vessels. The blood then carries the oxygen to parts of the body that need it.

When a fish gulps in water, muscles inside its mouth pump the water across two sets of internal gills and out of its gill slits. Some fish, such as sharks and mackerel, rely on ram breathing – they swim fast with their mouths open and this forces water past their gills.

After passing over its gills, water leaves this grouper through two flaps on its sides.

Gills for feeding

Many fish such as basking sharks and bream have rake-shaped gills. When water enters their mouths, these gill rakes trap floating food such as **plankton**. The fish then shake their gills to loosen the trapped food before sucking it down their throats.

Under pressure

Bony fish swim and float with the help of a **swim bladder**. This is a gas-filled sac (bag) found just below a fish's backbone. The swim bladder acts like a rubber ring to keep a fish **buoyant**.

Cartilaginous fish such as sharks have no swim bladder, but have a buoyant oily **liver** instead. Nevertheless, they need to keep swimming more of the time than bony fish to avoid sinking. Their tail fins are usually longer at the top than the bottom, which helps push them up in the water when they move their tails.

Water, water everywhere

If you eat something salty, your mouth feels dry because the salt sucks water out of it, and you need to drink more water. Fish that live in the sea need to drink a lot because the salt in the water around them sucks water out of their bodies. Fish that live in freshwater do not need to drink – their bodies contain more salt than the water around them. Their skin sucks in so much water that they need to wee almost all the time!

This *Beuthometes rubustus* is a bony fish. As it swims deeper, the **water pressure** around it increases, making its swim bladder smaller. This makes it less buoyant. To stop itself sinking when it stops, the fish then increases the amount of gas in its swim bladder.

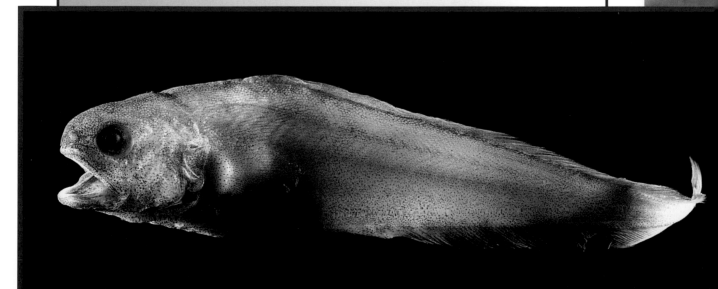

Perch-like fish

Perciformes – an **order** of bony fish – contains over 7000 different **species**. It gets its name from the perch, a typical member. All have similar anatomy (body construction). The characteristics they have in common include lots of small, sharp teeth and spiny and **cartilaginous** bones in their **fins**.

Variety

There are many distinct groups of perch-like fish, from bass and groupers to mackerel and wrasse. Gobies, blennies and weevers are generally small fish, often found in shallow seawater or rockpools. They have broad heads, thick lips and large eyes close together on top of their heads. Weevers spend much of their time buried in sand. The hard spines in their **dorsal** fins are filled with poison, which will sting any animal that grabs, lands or steps on them.

The smallest fish in the world

The tiniest of all fish is a perch relative. Adults of a goby (*Trimmatom nanus*) that lives around reefs in the Indian Ocean are less than 1 centimetre long.

dorsal fins

tail fin

pelvic fin

pectoral fin

Perciformes such as this freshwater perch usually have two dorsal fins, and their **pectoral** fins are positioned half-way up their sides. The **pelvic** fins under their stomach contain one spine.

Shoals of tuna hunt in big groups. When they spot prey they swim extra fast to catch it.

Hunters and hitchers

The biggest perch-like fish are ocean hunters of smaller fish. Tuna, swordfish and marlin can reach 900 kilograms in weight, and grow up to 4.5 metres long. They have special muscles that help them swim faster for longer than most fish. Groups of tuna swim together searching for **shoals** of **prey** such as anchovies. Swordfish and marlin have a long spike on their upper jaw, which they use to stun or injure their prey so they are easier to catch.

Remoras are a group of unusual perch-like fish. Instead of a dorsal fin they have a special sucker. They use this to hitch a ride on larger sea creatures, saving themselves the effort of swimming. Each species prefers a particular creature to ride on, be it whale, shark or turtle. Remoras also feed on bits of food dropped by their driver as it eats.

Fish in a freezer

The Antarctic icefish is a perch-like fish that can survive in the coldest water on Earth. Its blood does not freeze because it contains chemicals that act like antifreeze in a car radiator.

Freshwater fish

An easy way of looking at some of the many **orders** of bony fish is by grouping them according to where they live. Several orders of fish live almost always in freshwater.

The carp-like fish

Cypriniformes are carp-like fish. The smallest are brightly coloured tetras and the largest is the mahseer, a giant carp that lives in fast-flowing Himalayan rivers. All carp-like fish have **cartilaginous fin** bones, usually low **pectoral** fins and **pelvic** fins under their stomachs.

Many have special **adaptations** to help them feed. Carp, bream and goldfish have upper jaws that can extend to suck in food such as insect **larvae** that floats in the water or on the river or lake floor. They grind their food using special throat teeth before swallowing.

Unfair reputation

Red piranhas are small Cypriniformes with razor-sharp teeth that live in shoals in the River Amazon. They have a bad reputation that if an animal falls in the river, red piranhas will surround it and tear all the flesh off its bones. In fact, these fish mostly feed on other fish, nuts and seeds.

Loach are carp relatives that have finger-like barbels near their mouths. These barbels help them find food, such as worms, living amongst stones or in mud.

barbels

Fish out of water

The lungfish (order Dipteriformes) have **swim bladders** that act like lungs so they can survive dry seasons in parts of Africa and Australia. When the ponds they live in dry up, they bury themselves in mud and curl up in a cocoon (protective covering) of slime, with an airhole to breathe through. They slow down their breathing and can survive many months until rain comes. When the ground is wet enough, they leave their cocoon and slither to the nearest pond, where they can breathe using their **gills**.

All in a name

Catfish (order Siluriformes) have cartilaginous fin bones, **dorsal** fin spines and broad heads. They are called catfish because they have lots of **barbels** that look a bit like cats' whiskers. Catfish live in murky or muddy lake or river water.

Hardtongues (order Osteoglossiformes) are mostly tropical freshwater fish with large scales. They get their name from their toothed tongues that bite against rows of teeth on the base of their skull. They include the arapaima – the largest purely freshwater fish, at up to 5 metres long – that has scales tough enough to survive a caiman (freshwater alligator) attack. Elephant nose fish (order Mormyriformes) are so-called because they usually have long snouts, which they use to suck up food.

Elephant nose fish make electricity. They use it to find prey, a bit like a radar.

River and sea fish

Members of several fish **orders** spend part of their lives in freshwater and part in seawater, so they can spawn (lay their eggs) in just the right conditions. They sometimes travel immense distances over regular routes. This is called migration.

Breeding at sea

Eels (order Anguilliformes) are snake-like fish, usually without **pectoral** and **pelvic fins**, and with small **scales**. European eels spend most of their adult life living and feeding in European rivers. When they are about 10 years old they migrate up to 6000 kilometres downstream towards the sea, to reach a particular area of ocean near the USA. Here they spawn in the deep saltwater and then die.

Their eggs hatch and the large group of baby eels then migrate back to where their parents once lived. Sometimes they even wriggle for hundreds of metres across wet land to reach the right river. Once in the freshwater environment, they grow up fully to become adult eels, and the cycle continues.

*Baby eels have transparent skin and are often called glass eels. They migrate in **shoals** of many thousands.*

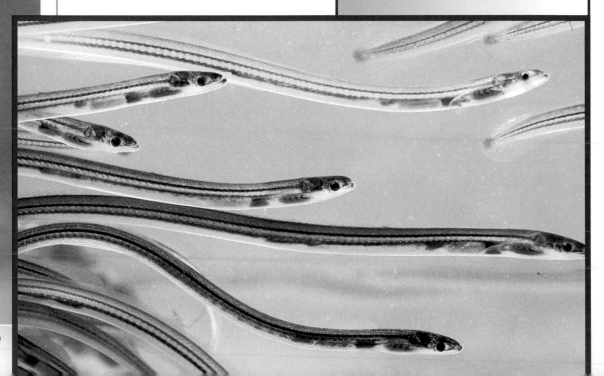

Breeding in rivers

The order Salmoniformes includes salmon, trout, char and pike. They all have scaleless heads and no spines in their fins. Pike have a **dorsal** fin near their tails, but salmon have an extra fatty fin behind their dorsal fin.

When they migrate, salmon often have to leap up rocky rapids to reach the right bit of river. In some spots bears wait to catch a meal.

Salmon spawn in rivers but live in the sea. Adults migrate from food-rich areas of sea to a particular river. They do this using the sun and stars at first, and then by following the taste of river water, which they remember from birth. Male salmon develop humped backs, hook-shaped jaws and red stripes on their sides to attract females. After spawning, many adults die, exhausted after their long trip. Their eggs hatch into young salmon that live for up to seven years in the river before going to sea.

Ancient fish

Sturgeons (order Acipenseriformes) have partly **cartilaginous** skeletons, **barbels** and bony plates rather than scales protecting their skin. **Fossils** suggest sturgeon have remained unchanged for millions of years. Some females spend 30 years at sea before they move into rivers to lay their first eggs.

Sea fish

Many different **orders** of fish spend their whole lives in shallow seas. Some roam over large areas in **shoals**, others live on or near the bottom.

Group living

Herring, sardine, pilchard and anchovy (order Clupeiformes) are classified together because they have forked tails, flattened silvery bodies and low **pectoral fins**. They all catch **plankton** to eat using their **gill** rakes (see box on page 10). Cod, hake, whiting and pollack (order Gadiformes) are larger fish with two or three **dorsal** fins and small **scales**. **Species** in both of these orders travel in large shoals of up to hundreds of thousands of individuals. All the fish in one shoal hatched from eggs at the same time, so they are all the same age and size.

Being one of many in a big shoal has its advantages. More eyes can spot danger earlier and groups have ways of protecting each other. If **predators** such as tuna attack a shoal of anchovy, the shoal often bunches together to form a vast writhing bait ball, sometimes hundreds of metres across. This confuses predators, who cannot easily spot a particular fish to chase, and makes it less likely for each individual fish to be killed.

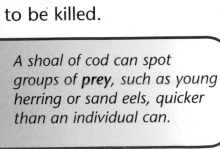

*A shoal of cod can spot groups of **prey**, such as young herring or sand eels, quicker than an individual can.*

On the surface

Flying fish (order Atheriniformes) are mostly **tropical** fish that live near the sea's surface. They have large pectoral (and sometimes also **pelvic**) fins positioned high on their bodies. These wing-like fins help them to glide or skip above water to get extra speed to escape predators.

Sunfish (order Tetraodontiformes) are massive, slow-swimming fish, up to 4 metres across, with no tail fin and long fins top and bottom. They have four teeth that form a beak to catch slippery food such as jellyfish. Their smaller relatives, pufferfish and porcupine fish, can puff up their spiky bodies with water to look bigger if a predator approaches.

On the bottom

Flatfish such as plaice, turbot, sole and flounder are classified in the order Pleuronectiformes. When they are babies their two eyes are on either side of their body, but as they develop, one eye moves to the other side. They spend much of their time lying flat on one side on the bottom of the sea. Having eyes on top allows them to spot a passing meal – such as shrimps – and approaching danger.

*When lying on the bottom, this dab stays hidden by burrowing into the sand and also by using its **camouflaged** skin to blend in.*

Shallow-water fish

Nearly 30 per cent of the world's fish **species** live in shallow waters near coasts and reefs. Tiny coral animals build rock-like reefs in shallow, warm **tropical** seawater. Many **orders** of fish live around reefs because there are lots of **prey** to catch and places to hide from danger.

Squirrelfish (order Beryciformes) are reef fish with large eyes and protruding lower jaws that make their faces look a bit like squirrels. Many live in crevices in reefs and come out to feed mostly at night. Their faded red colour is difficult to see in the dark water so they can hunt smaller fish more easily without being spotted.

The order Scorpaeniformes contains fish such as scorpionfish, stonefish and gurnards. They have bony ridges under their eyes on their large heads for armour and strong spines on their **dorsal fins**. Scorpionfish often have poison-filled spines for further protection from **predators**. They are brightly striped to warn other animals to avoid their sting. Stonefish are masters of disguise – they lie half-buried in sand, their spiny bodies cloaked with seaweed, waiting to ambush prey.

*Gurnards have sensitive finger-like bones in their **pectoral** fins that they use to walk along and to find buried food such as small crabs.*

Seahorses, pipefish and sticklebacks

Fish classified in the order Gasterosteiformes have ridged, armoured bodies with no scales. They have tube-shaped heads and mostly small fins. Some sticklebacks live in shallow seawater. The fifteen-spined stickleback is so-named because of the fifteen short, sharp spines in front of its dorsal fin. The male builds a small nest out of seaweed for the female to lay her eggs in.

Pipefish and seahorses swim weakly using mostly their dorsal fin. Pipefish are shaped like long pipes and seahorses have an angled, horse-shaped head. Seahorses coil their tail around seaweed to hold on if the water is moving or if they want a rest. A female lays her eggs in a special pouch on the male's stomach. Then the male looks after the eggs until they hatch.

Some seahorses such as the pygmy seahorse of Indonesia are brightly coloured for **camouflage** amongst bright coral. Others such as the sea dragon are covered in ragged skin to make them look like floating seaweed.

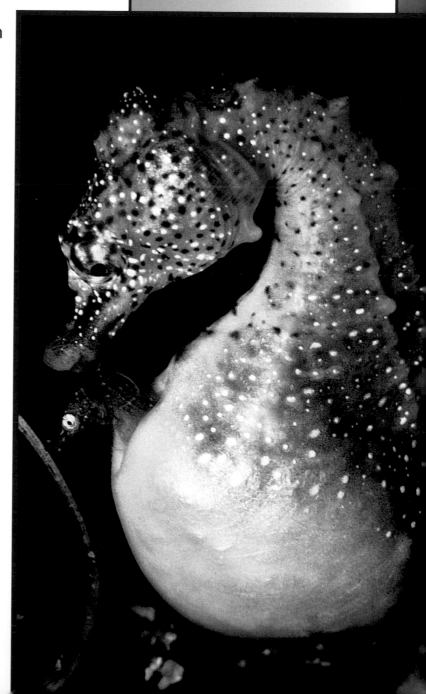

When baby seahorses have hatched from their eggs, they leave the safety of their father's pouch.

Deep-sea fish

Life in the deepest oceans is very demanding. The weight of all the water above means that there is great **water pressure** in the deep. At several kilometres below the surface, water is very cold and almost completely dark. Deep-sea fish need special **adaptations** to be able to live there, such as large eyes to sense any light so far from the surface.

Seeing the light

Many deep-sea fish make their own light using special chemicals. Lantern fish (**order** Myctophiformes) have rows of lights on their sides that flash on and off. These act as a signal to other lantern fish, so they can remain close together. The lights also attract their **prey** such as prawns and small fish, which they catch in shallower waters at night.

Anglerfish (order Lophiiformes) have loose scaleless skin, large heads and mouths with sharp teeth. They have a long **dorsal fin** bone with a dangling blob of skin at its end that produces light. The fish folds this forward like an angler's rod and uses the light as bait to attract prey towards its mouth.

The Atlantic football fish has a ball-shaped head. Its 'rod' is folded back as it swims.

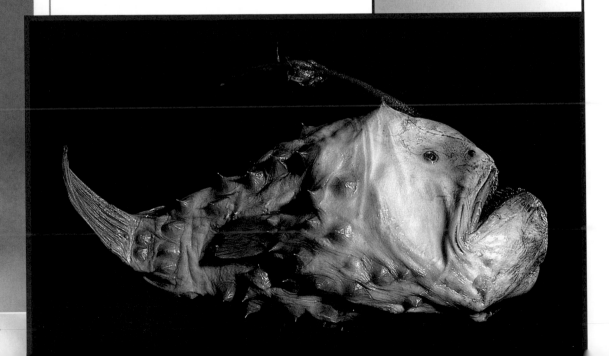

Grabbing a meal

There is such a shortage of food in the depths that fish living there have to be certain of catching any meal that is going. Several orders of fish spend most of their time on the bottom searching for food. Spiny eels (order Notacanthiformes) have bony

Deep sea gulper eels (order Sacchopharyngiformes) can measure up to 2 metres long, but their jaws are big enough to swallow prey larger than themselves. They need to eat big meals as they may have to wait a long time for the next one.

heads, long, tapering bodies and **larvae** a bit like those of shallow water eels. They swim head-down along the bottom until they find starfish to eat.

Hatchetfish (order Stomiiformes) are shaped a bit like a small axe. They have big, upturned mouths and large eyes to see and catch food moving towards them from the lighter waters above. Viperfish and dragon fish, their relatives, have fangs that are so long they cannot close their mouths. Both these fish attract prey by making light and then swim fast to spear their meal before swallowing it. Dragon fish make a special red light to spot their prey. The prey cannot see this light, so the dragon fish can sneak up on them.

Sharks

Sharks range from 10-metre-long whale sharks weighing 20 tonnes down to small dogfish. They have some of the most notorious jaws in the oceans, but they are not made of bone. Sharks (**order** Selachii) are one of three orders within the **class** Chondrichthyes – the **cartilaginous** fish.

Bone and skin

Shark skin is covered in pointed **scales**. The scales interlock a bit like chainmail armour to protect sharks from damage and to make make them streamlined. Sharks have five or seven **gill** slits on each side of their body, unlike bony fish which only have one on each side. Sharks all have a cartilage skeleton. Their jaw is loosely connected to their skull, which means they can stretch their mouths forward to bite. Their **fins** are fleshy and typically their tail fins are longer on top.

*This great white shark, like all sharks, remains **buoyant** because its massive **liver** – up to a quarter of its body weight – is full of lightweight oils.*

A headstart

Unlike most fish, the eggs of some shark **species** hatch inside and they give birth to live young. Others such as the bullhead shark lay their delicate eggs in protective capsules, often called mermaids' purses. These purses are split open and discarded by the young once the eggs hatch.

Shark teeth

Shark teeth grow in two or three rows. Rows of new, sharp teeth move forward out of the jaw – a bit like a tooth conveyor belt – to replace any worn or broken ones at the front. The teeth vary in shape and size. Sharks like the sandtiger have slender and hook-shaped teeth to catch fish. Smoothhounds and others have blunt teeth for crushing **prey** such as crabs. Those like the great white shark have triangular and dagger-shaped teeth to cut the flesh of larger prey. Several sharks such as basking and whale sharks have tiny teeth – they feed on the **plankton** they catch using their gill rakes (see box on page 10).

Feeding habits

Sharks vary widely in the way they catch prey. The megamouth swims with its massive mouth open, feeding on deep-sea plankton. The great white shark is a fast-swimming **predator** of large fish and sea mammals such as whales. The sawfish has a long, flat snout with large, tooth-like scales along the sides – it looks a bit like a chainsaw – that it slashes through **shoals** of fish.

The head shape of these sharks led to their common name – hammerhead. Scientists believe this shape is associated with the hammerhead's method of sensing hidden prey, which works a bit like a metal detector.

Shark cartilage

Cartilage is a tough body material that is softer than bone but lighter and more flexible. A shark's backbone and jaws are extra strong for swimming and biting because the cartilage is strengthened by tiny, hard crystals that make it less bendy.

Rays and skates (**order** Rajiformes) are close relatives of sharks. They are grouped separately from sharks because they have flattened bodies with eyes on top and spend much of their time lying on the sea floor. They swim by flapping their wide **pectoral fins** a bit like wings.

Unlike flatfish, their **gill** slits and mouth are underneath. As their mouths are flat against the ground, they have holes behind their eyes where they suck in water to flow over the gills inside.

Skates and rays usually have a whip-like tail and often have spiny skin. The skin on top is commonly patterned to look like the seafloor or to change the shape of their outline. This **camouflage** helps them hide from **predators** but also helps them catch their own **prey**. They often lie partly buried in sand and flop over prey such as flatfish, crabs and clams to catch them. Stingrays have a long, sharp spine just above their tail that contains poison for defence if they are attacked or accidentally trodden on.

You can see the mouth and gill slits on the underside of this stingray.

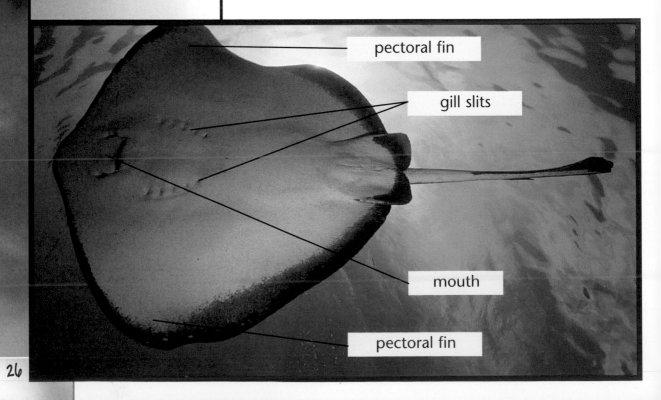

pectoral fin

gill slits

mouth

pectoral fin

Big brother

The Rajiformes are usually up to 1 metre across. The manta ray is an exception – it can reach 9 metres across and weigh a tonne. It feeds on areas of **plankton** or small fish in **tropical** waters. Manta rays swim in slow somersaults through their food source and use the large flaps in front of their eyes as paddles to funnel plankton into their open mouths.

Jawless fish

Most fish in the world have jaws but there is one **class** that does not. It is called the Agnatha, or jawless fish, and groups lampreys (order Petromyzoniformes) and hagfish (order Myxiniformes). These fish have small **cartilaginous** skeletons, no scales and eel-like bodies. Without jaws to open and close their mouth, they have to suck in their food from other fish. Lampreys attach themselves to other fish using their mouths. Circles of teeth scrape the skin of their carrier and they suck in the blood. Hagfish have sharp spikes on their tongues to grate bits of flesh off dead or dying animals, even fish caught in nets. They are blind and find food using their sense of smell and their **barbels**.

*Hagfish can produce lots of sticky slime from holes in their skin to put off **predators**.*

All sorts of fish

This book has covered just some of the very different shapes, sizes and ways of life of fish. However different they are, most fish share several basic characteristics:

- they swim with **fins**, float with the help of a **swim bladder** or oily **liver** and are shaped to move through the water easily
- they breathe using **gills**
- their young hatch from eggs
- their skin is covered with **scales**.

Variations on a theme

These characteristics vary in each fish **species**, often because of their way of life. For example, most fish lay lots of eggs in the water and leave them to hatch out on their own unprotected. Some sharks, though, give their eggs a headstart, by keeping them safely inside their bodies until they hatch. As this uses up energy, and there is limited space inside their bodies, they cannot produce many eggs this way.

Different fish species look the way they do mostly because of their way of life – from where they live to how they feed and reproduce.

Looking like a fish

An animal is not a fish unless it has all the right characteristics. In spite of their names, jellyfish and starfish are not fish because they lack most fish characteristics – they do not have skeletons, scales or fins. It is trickier to tell that other animals are not fish. Tadpoles hatch from soft eggs, breathe using gills and use fins on their tails to swim. On close inspection they have no scales, but it is much easier to see they are not fish when they start to change into adult frogs!

Although fish classification is sometimes tricky, it is an extremely useful way of learning more about the different groups of fascinating fish around the world.

Seasnakes look a bit like eels, swim in the sea, lay eggs and have scales. However, they are not fish because, amongst other reasons, they do not have gills.

The same solution

Fish classified in different **orders** sometimes show great similarities in characteristics because of their way of life. For example, sole (bony fish) and skates (**cartilaginous**) are both flat in shape and have **camouflaged** skin so they can hide and feed on the seafloor.

Glossary

adaptation special feature that helps living things to survive in their particular habitat e.g. gills and fins

barbels fleshy, sensitive whiskers

buoyant able to float

camouflage colour, shape or pattern, that helps an animal hide in its environment

cartilage firm but flexible skeleton material

cartilaginous having cartilage rather than bone

class classification grouping. There are three classes of fish, each containing several orders.

descendant later generation of an organism. You are a descendant of your grandparents.

dorsal in or attached to the back

family classification grouping. Herrings are a family of bony fish.

fin flap of skin that helps a fish swim

fossil remains of an organism that once lived on Earth

genus (plural **genera**) classification grouping. In each family of fish there are usually several genera.

gills structures used for breathing underwater

larvae young hatched from egg

liver body organ that cleans the blood

order classification grouping. There are three orders within the class of cartilaginous fish.

organ part of body with a specific and important job to do, such as the liver or heart

organism living thing

pectoral in or attached to the chest bones

pelvic in or attached to the hipbones

phylum (pural **phyla**) classification grouping. Each phylum is divided into different classes.

plankton tiny animals and plants that float in water

predator animal that hunts and eats other animals

prey animal that is hunted and eaten by another animal

reproduce have babies

scales overlapping or interlocking pieces that form a protective layer over fish skin

shoal group of fish

species classification grouping. A species is a particular type of organism, such as a turbot.

suckle feed young at the breast or shoulder

swim bladder gas-filled sac (bag) inside bony fish that helps keep them buoyant

tropical found in the Tropics (near the equator, where it is warmest)

vertebrate animal with an internal backbone

water pressure weight of water pushing against an organism's body

Further resources

Books
A Whale is not Fish: And other Animal Mix-ups, Melvin Burger (Scholastic, 1996)

Collins Pocket Guide: Fish, Peter Miller and Mick Loates (Harper Collins, 1997)

Extraordinary Fish, Francis Dipper (BBC Books, 2001)

Eyewitness Guide: Fish, Steve Parker (Dorling Kindersly, 1990)

Fish Facts, Geoffrey Swinney and Kate Charlesworth (National Museum of Scotland, 1991)

The Blue Planet, Andrew Byatt and others (BBC Books, 2001) (also available as videos of TV series)

The Encyclopedia of Aquarium Fish, ed. Dick Mills and John Tullock (David and Charles, 2001)

Websites
Natural History Museum:
www.nhm.ac.uk

Seafish and other marine creatures:
www.bbc.co.uk/nature/blueplanet/webs/index.shtml

Simple fish facts:
www.fishid.com/facts.htm

Shark information:
www.animalnation.com/Archive/aqua/Aqu.html
www.sdnhm.org/kids/sharks/index.html

Places to visit
Visit national aquariums such as the National Marine Aquarium in Plymouth, UK, or the National Aquarium, Canberra, Australia, or private aquaria in zoos, wildlife collections and larger suppliers of fish for home aquaria. Fishmarkets and harbours are also good places to visit to see the range of different fish.

Index